The Art of Selling

The Secrets that Top Sellers Don't Want You to Know About Increasing Sales, Income, and Profits

© **Copyright 2016 by Lifestyle Initiative, Inc. - All rights reserved.**

This document is geared towards providing exact and reliable information in regards to the topic and issue covered. The publication is sold with the idea that the publisher is not required to render accounting, officially permitted, or otherwise, qualified services. If advice is necessary, legal or professional, a practiced individual in the profession should be ordered.

From a Declaration of Principles which was accepted and approved equally by a Committee of the American Bar Association and a Committee of Publishers and Associations.

In no way is it legal to reproduce, duplicate, or transmit any part of this document in either electronic means or in printed format. Recording of this publication is strictly prohibited and any storage of this document is not allowed unless with written permission from the publisher. All rights reserved.

The information provided herein is stated to be truthful and consistent, in that any liability, in terms of inattention or otherwise, by any usage or abuse of any policies, processes, or directions contained within is the solitary and utter responsibility of the recipient reader. Under no circumstances will any legal responsibility or blame be held against the publisher for any reparation, damages, or monetary loss due to the information herein, either directly or indirectly.

Respective authors own all copyrights not held by the publisher.

The information herein is offered for informational purposes solely, and is universal as so. The presentation of the information is without contract or any type of guarantee assurance.

The trademarks that are used are without any consent, and the publication of the trademark is without permission or backing by the trademark owner. All trademarks and brands within this book are for clarifying purposes only and are the owned by the owners themselves, not affiliated with this document.

Table of Contents

Table of Contents..4

Introduction...5

Chapter 1 - Brush Up On Your Selling Principles..7

Chapter 2 - Prospects Buy For Their Own Reasons..29

Chapter 3 - Create A Prospective Attitude........43

Chapter 4 - Treat The Prospect or Customer With Importance......................................57

Chapter 5 - Making Use Of Elevator Statements..71

Chapter 6 - Always Have A 'Closing' Attitude...85

Conclusion..100

Introduction

Was there ever a time when a sales person approached you and tried to sell you their product? What was your reaction? Were you quick to agree to everything the sales person said, or buy the product he or she was selling? It is with absolute certainty that your initial reaction was to put your guard up and not take the sales person's word for it.

Trying to get a person to make that buying decision is one of the hardest things in the world to pull off. It has been every sales person's struggle; to be able to get a person to trust them and see the benefits of what they are selling, and then buy.

Contrary to what most people believe, selling is not something that is hard to master. With the right attitude and mindset, a sales person will be able to help people with their problem and at the same time create a business.

This book is about the techniques involved on how to achieve just that; a successful sales career. This book will teach you the secrets that top sales people don't want you to know about increasing sales, income, and profits.

Chapter 1 - Brush Up On Your Selling Principles

Not only is it important for a sales person to study and master specific techniques in selling, but it is also important to understand the why of that sales technique. That enables you to internalize the information, and then make it your own. We want to share with you specific selling principles that will explain the why behind the sales techniques you'll be learning.

One of the principles that should guide you in your sales career is this: Selling is a process, not an event. Even if your sales cycle is short, it's not an event based on luck; it's a planned process. You're a professional sales person, which means you go into all sales calls prepared.

You should know your sales process and where you are in that process with each of your prospects. You should also know what needs to be done to move to the next step. By following a road map, if you will, you will know what needs to happen to move the decision forward.

Do you have a process that you follow every time? Or do you let your prospect move you towards whatever he wants to do and hope that he makes a positive buying decision? To be professional in selling, you need to know what the steps are in the purchasing cycle, and you need to know how to move someone through those steps.

Do not leave it up to chance. You have to have a procedure that you need to follow each and every time. This process will obviously need some flexibility, but it is a routine that you practice and master so that you can make every conversation with a prospect count. Selling should involve a relationship between you and your prospect. You need to take the time to get to know the prospect; what he wants and needs and why he wants and needs those things.

Selling is not something that you do TO someone. It is something you do WITH someone. As the relationship between prospect and sales person grow, you learn how you may be able to solve a problem your prospect has with one of your products or services.

Selling is also the motivated, energetic, and dynamic seeking of customers or prospects with the intent of addressing their needs. To become successful at selling, one must develop and demonstrate active listening skills. Without them, it is impossible for a seller to find the customer or prospect's need.

A successful seller must also learn how to show confidence in presenting his product or service. In addition, sellers must show a certain level of competency with regard to in-depth product or service details. In other words, sellers rely in the prospect or customer's perception of their excellence and/or their expertise at all times.

As sellers, you must also learn how to make exciting "moments of truth" for the customer or prospect, even though chances are slim that they will go through with the order. Selling is, in some way, similar to Marketing. Both of them aims to make all interactions with your company a great experience.

Know the True Definition of the Word "Prospect"

All throughout this book, we will mention the word "prospect" countless times. So the question is, what is a prospect? We ask the question because there is a difference between a "suspect" and a "prospect."

Suspects have the potential to be prospects; but you don't know yet. A prospect has a need for the product, a possible desire to own the product, and the financial capability to implement that decision. Remember this: You spend time with suspects, and you invest time with prospects.

Right now, your goal is to create a profile of your ideal prospect. This is necessary so that you can identify the characteristics and demographics surrounding those that you have already closed, and then look for similar entities to do business with. For example, if within your existing customer-base your best customers are in a certain geographical area, you owe it to yourself to explore other opportunities in the same geographic area.

The same will hold true if they belong to a trade association. Everyone else in that association would be a warm market for you. Taking the time to find this information is important. So what does the ideal prospect look like for you? To create this profile, you need to begin to think about your current customers.

What similarities can you see in them? Do they have the same job title? Or are they from the same industry? Are they companies? Do they all have the same size or location? Remember, when you are building the profile of an ideal prospect, you must consider the company as well as yourself. Would this type of customer be the most profitable to the company or for you to have a sale?

You need to make sure you are targeting the customers who give you the best return on your time invested. Once you identify a prospect that fits the profile of a good customer of yours, you must contact that prospect with the intention of asking enough questions so that you can either:

1. Turn him from a suspect to a prospect, or
2. Disqualify him as a prospect and move on, or
3. Find the real buyer or decision maker, or
4. Sell your Products

Keep in mind that a truly qualified prospect should meet all these qualifications. They have the authority to buy, the ability to pay, and an unmet need. It's important not to push products on people who are not qualified prospects. It wastes time, and damages their trust in you and your company.

It is better to disqualify a prospect and move on. To better identify qualified prospects, create profiles of your best customers and begin to look for prospects that fit that profile. Realize of course that there are some prospects who buy that don't fit that profile.

Use the profile as a sort of magnifying glass to zero in on the best people to spend your time with. Even if you think that you have the best product or service in the world, there are people out there who couldn't care less. Your job is to eliminate them quickly so you can help the people who do need what you sell. If you keep eliminating the NOs, you have more time for the YESs.

Be the Solution to the Customer's Problem

This is another crucial principle that every budding sales professional should keep in mind. You make more money solving problems than you do by selling your products or services. When you always sell products instead of solving problems, you create frustration and short-term customers. But when you listen to the prospect and understand their problem, and then offer a solution to that problem, you become extremely valuable to your prospect.

Here is an example: Let's say that you saw a prospect while attending a car show. Now you know that this customer must love cars and there is a big chance that he is a car owner himself. You, being a sales professional for a car painting service, approaches the prospect and begin to make a sales pitch.

Do you think you will be successful in closing the sale with that prospect? No. Because as it turns out, the prospect is not having any issues with the paint on his car. Instead, his main issue with his car is that it always leaks oil.

Now here comes another sales professional who offers car services which specifically addresses oil leaks. He makes a sales pitch to the prospect and successfully closes the sale. Why? Because the second sales professional was able to address a specific problem or need of the prospect.

By solving your prospect's needs, you will be able to get more referrals and more loyal customers. Not only should you learn how to solve a current problem, you must also learn how to anticipate the prospect's needs. Anticipating needs or problems sells more products and satisfies more customers.

For example, let's say that you have a prospect who recently bought a car. As an automobile tire salesman, you approach him and begin to make your sales pitch about how great your tires are and how it can prevent dangerous accidental skids.

Now here comes a second sales professional who sells oil changing and engine maintenance services. Who do you think has a greater chance of closing the sale?

The one who has a greater chance of closing the sale would be the second sales professional of course. Why? Because tires are the last thing to worry about with a brand new car. The second sales professional was able to anticipate that the first thing car owners must address with a brand new car is engine maintenance and an oil change once they reach their first thousand kilometers. He was able to anticipate that need because he knew that the car is still in its "engine break in" stage.

If customers could solve their own problems, they wouldn't need you. If you frame what you sell in terms of solutions, then you become an expert in their eyes. You see, you are doing your customer a great service by providing them with the benefits of what you sell. If you are thinking about the money you will make from the sale and what you would do with it, then your chances of closing the sale will significantly decrease. Remember, selling IS solving.

Sell with Integrity and Honesty

Over the years, sales people have been given a bad reputation of being dishonest and unethical. A truly professional sales person, with their goal on a long-term career in sales, realize that honesty--

ethical dealings with others--is the only way to build a solid career.

We hear story after story of people who did the right thing, and were rewarded for it somewhere down the line. We are also reminded of a sales manager who sent out an inexperienced sales person. The rookie came back with a $225 check for what should have been $125. The manager, of course, quickly took the rookie back to the customer, explained the mistake, and then offered to give them the service for free. The man gladly accepted the offer and then went on to sign up for a $100 monthly service contract.

Now if the manager had not rectified the first mistake of $225, the customer probably would have done some shopping around and found someone more reasonable to give his $1200 a year business to. In the long run, it pays to be honest and straightforward with your prospects and customers. Being ethical is not only the right way to live, it's also the most pragmatic way to live.

A true sales professional not only talks about ethics, but he or she also lives ethically. In this day and age, people are searching for people they can trust. Because it is a cynical time, you have to understand that most of the people you deal with for the first time have their guard up. They want to make sure that you can be trusted.

This is when a sterling reputation can help you out. You can give references of other customers that will attest to your honesty and your honest way of doing business. And because you have confidence in your product and possess the knowledge that you conduct your life in a fair and honest nature, you could look that prospect right in the eye and exude the warmth and assurance that you are to be trusted.

As a sales professional looking to make an illustrious career, it is of utmost importance that you maintain a reputation of trustworthiness. Show people that you can be trusted and you can bet your bottom dollar that the prospects or customers will seek you out themselves. If have a flawless reputation, they will seek you out by name and always come to you every time they need a product or service that could help them in taking care of a problem.

Be a Positive Thinking Salesman

Unfortunately, there's a lot of confusion about positive thinking. Some people say, "..with a positive attitude you can just do anything." That simply is not true. It won't let you do anything, but it will let you do everything better than negative thinking will.

Here's one simple example. Michael Jordan is a great athlete. But even with his athleticism, and even if he was a great positive thinker, he still would make a terrible singer. What we're talking about here is positive thinking based on specific reasons for that optimistic hope. It is ridiculous and frustrating for a new sales person to have his manager say, "go get `em." or "I know you can do it" and then send them out with no training or direction.

That leads to frustration and failure. The student must be a constant learner. Preparation will develop a positive attitude to go out and succeed. Remember, your business is never good or bad out there. It's either good or bad between your own two ears. There are many examples of sales people who are very successful in what is supposedly a down market; a sluggish industry. Don't listen to the naysayers. Keep your attitude up and your sales will follow. There are three action steps you can take to be a positive thinker:

1. Accept the fact that only you can control your attitude. Your attitude is not governed by the prospect of the manager who doesn't support you or the economist who predict gloom and doom in your career. You must take control of your own attitude and develop an optimistic sense of success.

2. Make sure you commit to doing whatever is necessary to keep in control of your attitude. Say positive affirmations, take a brisk walk around the block, or do whatever steps that work for you to maintain or regain your commitment to taking control.

3. Read something of value to you personally and professionally for at least 20 minutes every day. Read something that inspires or educate.

These simple steps will help you keep your attitude in the right frame of mind, so that you can be free to be a problem solver for your prospects. If your prospect says NO, don't take it personally. Be a positive thinker and think that maybe the reason why the prospect said no is because he is currently encountering financial issues.

If so, present him with payment terms that will ease--not add--to his financial burden. If the prospect keeps on hesitating to finalize the order, be a positive thinker and think maybe the reason for the stall is because he doesn't have enough information yet to go through the closing of the sale. Never take things personally.

If a prospect rejects your offer, know that he or she is rejecting it not because of you, but because he hasn't realized that he needs the product yet. Be enthusiastic each time you approach a prospect, even though you have been rejected countless times by that same prospect. Once you master the art of thinking positive, you'll exude confidence in every sales call.

Chapter 2 - Prospects Buy For Their Own Reasons

If there's one thing about a prospect's mindset that most novice sales professionals forget, it is the fact that prospects purchase for their reasons, not yours. Your reason for selling is probably to make a commission. But the customer purchases for their own reasons, not your reasons.

Reasons are defined as motives, feelings, and benefits that move people to take action. Reasons are different from benefits. You need to ask questions to discover the reason why your prospects may want your product or service. Be aware, however, that when you probe the prospect for the first time, you'll get an answer the person thinks you want to hear. The second time you probe, you will get an answer that someone very near to that person would like to hear. The third time you probe, you may just get the truth.

Most people are not trying to be deceitful. They just haven't given much thought to what really is important to them. You see, people purchase for emotional and logical reasons. Your job is to discover both kinds of reasons by asking questions.

Don't you ever get annoyed when sales people in a store approaches you and starts telling you about how great this product is, or how many people are buying it right now? It is most likely that you're annoyed because of two things:

The sales person in the store is presenting you a product that you're not even interested in, and they're presenting it to you in the most persistent—and extremely annoying—manner.

You have no reason to buy that particular product hence the non-interest. The same thing applies with your prospect. They will never, ever buy something without any specific reason. Not unless your prospect is a multi-millionaire and is just splurging cash.

And even if the customer is interested in the product and there's probable reason to buy, they won't buy it right away. Why? Well, maybe there's something that's making them hesitate. Maybe they don't like the price or the quality of the product. Quality and Product are both valid reasons to consider before making a purchase.

A skilled sales professional will always try to uncover a need and make the prospect realize that there is indeed a reason for him to buy the service or product. Think of it as making a light bulb go off in the prospect or customer's head when they come to a realization. So how do you uncover a need and make the prospect realize that there's a reason to make the purchase? Well, it all starts by asking questions.

Help them find their reason to buy the product or service by asking them questions. As you ask questions, both you and the prospect will realize the need for the service or product and whether there's an urgency to fulfill that need. Once you show your prospect that there's a reason to consider what you're offering, the prospect themselves will be the one to seek you out and ask for your product or service. Uncovering the reason and making the prospect realize that they indeed have a valid reason to go through with the sale is one of the basic skills that you must learn in order to be an extremely successful sales professional.

Prospects Buy What the Product Does for Them, Not the Product Itself

Prospects don't buy your products and services. They buy what your products and services will do for them. It's true that people have different reasons--as in the last principle. But this principle focuses on the benefits they realize as a result of owning the product.

If you sell mattresses for example, the benefit might be there's room to stretch or get a good night's sleep. It doesn't matter what you think the benefit of the product is. What matters is what the prospect thinks the benefits are. So the next time someone asks you, "what do you sell?" Answer, in terms of a benefit instead of a product.

Here's an example: Let's say that there are two sales professional attending a mattress convention. A prospect comes to the convention looking for a mattress that will fit him and his wife, and also make sure that he doesn't get any backaches when he wakes up in the morning.

The prospect approaches sales person number A and asks him, "What are you selling?" Sales person A then tells the prospect that he sells quality mattresses made of soft fabric and high-quality springs that gives that bouncy feel when someone lies down on it. The prospect then approaches sales person B and asks the same thing. Sales person B, however, tells the prospect that he's selling mattresses that offer comfortability, affordability, and quality.

The mattress offers comfortability by having quality material, which eliminates back aches, affordability in a sense that the cost to buy and maintain the mattress is extremely low, and lastly, quality since it will not exhibit any wear and tear even with excessive use. So who do you think the prospect will buy the mattress from? If your answer is sales person B, then you are correct. Why? Because sales person B presented what the product does for the customer instead of what the product is.

Leading with what a product does will pique your prospect's interest, since he is specifically looking for those benefits. Not only will you attract more prospects by leading with the benefit of your product or service, but also increase your chance of closing the sale significantly. Again, why your prospect wants the particular product is uncovered by asking questions.

If a customer or a prospect comes to you and asks, "What do you sell?" Ask them a question first. Ask them why they need that product or service, and then relate the need with your product's benefits. Do not be afraid to ask your prospect questions. Because only with questions do you find the prospect's reason to buy and make them realize the urgency at which they need to get the product. Remember, lead with the need and sell with great speed.

Don't Fear Rejection

Research has shown that 63% of all sales interviews end with no direct effort to close the sale. The sales person is comfortable building rapport, asking questions to find the need, and even presenting the offer. But because of a fear of rejection, they talk and talk but never ask for the order.

Are you a professional sales person, or are you a professional visitor? Those sales people who have a poor attitude about themselves will have to admit that they have a hard time facing up to rejection. After making a rather spectacular presentation, you find yourself out on the street with no order, no signed paperwork, and nothing to show for your efforts. Those with a bad attitude about themselves will have to go to the closest coffee shop and lick their wounds and have a pity party about how cruel the world can be.

However, those with a healthy attitude will find themselves out on the street after a NO, shake it off, and go about finding the next prospect to whom they can make their presentation. This also relates to positive thinking. Once you get rejected, think positive and move on to the next prospect.

There is a direct bearing over a sales person's self image and their self success. Sales people who have a healthy self image; not conceit but a healthy self-acceptance of their own faults, their shortcomings, and their own strengths can go from one prospect to the next many times and almost regardless of the reception they get. However, let's admit it. There's a limit to how much rejection anyone can stand. The point is, never ever let rejection pull you down.

When you improve your attitude about yourself, in other words improve your self-image, you will improve your sales performance. There are many ways you can improve your attitude about yourself. Here are two action steps you can take:

1. Dress the part - It is proven that we feel better about ourselves when we are dressed for success. Make sure you are putting your best foot forward by keeping your shoes shined, your hair neat, and your clothes spick and span. Surely you're not expecting a prospect to trust a sales person who looks like they just jumped out of a dumpster.

Always dress like a professional; that you're a well respected, trusted sales person.

2. Become an expert in your chosen profession of selling - Learn the sales techniques that work best in your selling situation. And practice them until they become a part of you. With improved effectiveness, your love for selling would be even greater, because an important key to maintaining a good attitude is to know what you are doing. Besides, no prospect would trust a sales person who does not know the Do's and Dont's of selling. Learn you craft and learn them good. Become a master of your field; an expert. We

all know that everybody runs to the expert if things go sour.

Chapter 3 - Create a Prospective Attitude

No matter how good you are at building rapport, uncovering needs and wants, asking questions, asking for the order, managing objections, making your presentation or your product knowledge, you're out of business if you don't have a prospect. Prospecting is one of the most important keys to your success. So when should you be prospecting? Well, the answer is all the time.

Prospecting is not an eight to five job. Prospecting, when performed amicably, can be done in essentially any setting; in social gatherings, in an airport, on an airplane, at a club meeting or during lunchtime. In general, wherever people are present is an opportunity to prospect. This doesn't necessarily mean you approach everyone at the party, corner the people on the driving range, speak to every person at the post office or in line at the fast food place.

The successful prospecting attitude does mean, however, that when great prospectors pick up the newspaper, there is a sensitivity to local events or news stories that contain leads or prospects for the business. The successful prospecting attitude means tuning in to conversations that would directly, or indirectly, involve the use of the product or service you offer.

Pay attention to the events, trends, conversations, and your current customers. Regularly get out of the networking circles you're in and start another circle or chain. Don't let your courier depend on one specific group of individuals.

How do you prospect? First, you must develop a genuine interest in other people. Open up a friendly conversation about something you're both experiencing and begin listening to the other person. In the conversation you may find out that you have a product or service they would need, or at least get a chance to tell them what you do.

Discover a way, in a quick sentence or two, to pique someone's interest. Have you ever had the experience that when you bought a certain car, say a red Ford, and then wherever you look you saw red

Fords? It's the same thing with prospecting. If you're thinking about prospects and looking for them wherever you go, you will surely find them.

To be an effective prospector, make it a point to speak to at least two new people that you don't know. Strike up a conversation and see where it leads you. It will take some practice to become comfortable and effective at this, but what a great benefit to have a full pipeline of prospects.

Having a stable pipeline of prospects allows you to focus on spending time with them and addressing their need, instead of spending countless hours or even days looking for one. Always find opportunities to discuss your business without coming off as being too pushy or suggestive. Remember, every person you encounter is an opportunity for you to not only help them with a need, but also develop a long lasting relationship. One that could prove beneficial to both you and your customer.

Know Where to Get Quality Prospects

Prospects come from many lead sources. It's important that you know your best lead sources. Some categories include:

1. Existing customers - These are the people who you are currently dealing with. The usual question that comes into mind when dealing with existing customers is, are they willing to buy more or different products from you? This is

considered as one of the best sources of leads. Since they already bought a product or service from you, you've already built rapport with these customers and it only takes a slight shove in the right direction for them to make another purchase.

2. Referrals - These are a great lead source because you go into the process with an introduction from someone else. These usually come from existing customers, or customers who have no need of your services or products, but knows a friend, a colleague, or a family member who does.

3. A warm market - This is your family, your friends, your colleagues, former customers; people you know personally and have already developed a rapport and trust. This is usually the lead source most novice sales professionals take their prospects from. The reason being is that since you already developed rapport and trust, the chances of them buying from you is high.

4. A niche market or related industry - This is a business that you're competing against, but is what you sell into. In other words, you and the sales person at that business can

team up to offer an excellent full service package. Of course, you may be lucky enough to work for a business that has a marketing effort that generates leads for you. Think of this as having a symbiotic relationship with competition.

5. Cold calling - This is done best through your observation of new business openings in newspaper articles, or other such current events. But sometimes, it's just getting a list of people and starting to dial the phone.

Of all these lead sources, which are the ones that work best for you? To be able to find out your finest lead sources, write down on a piece of paper the five categories that we've mentioned and estimate the percentage of your prospects that come from each of those sources. 35% of most sales people's prospects come from existing customers, 15% through referrals, 5% through what we call "warm" market, 5% through a niche market, 30% through their marketing efforts, and 10 % through the cold calls that they make.

By doing this, on your own, you can find out your situation and you can see where your prospects are coming from. Now realize that not all of these categories give you qualified prospects. So identify which categories are at the top; those two categories that are at the top you turn prospects into qualified buyers and into customers. In order to grow your business, you must handle your leads or your prospects efficiently. The point is to invest time and effort on the prospects that yield you the highest returns.

Perform Pipeline Planning

Successful sales professionals understand that having prospects to call on is an important part of the selling cycle. This process is called "Pipeline planning." Having a steady supply of leads based on probability of "close" ensures the sales professional is managing the future as well as the present.

Pipeline planning requires understanding and categorizing your prospects by metrics that are important to you and your business. It would need to include the name, primary contact, contact information, probability of close, and type of customer; either new or existing. Take your current prospects and list them on paper.

The probability of close could mean you would put an "A" beside a prospect that you think would close in less than 30 days. A "B" based on the probability you will close in less than 60 days. And a "C" based on thinking the close will happen in less than 90 days.

You can adjust the timeline to fit your specific situation or selling cycle. This list, when filled out, would give you an opportunity to look at a projection of your activities and ensure that you have enough qualified leads to work on every single day. There are many kinds of software out there that can keep all pertinent information.

You could also do what every successful salesman did before these software advancements came to be: they took an old-fashioned 3x5 card, wrote their top 20 accounts on it, then worked on those accounts until they said no or wrote up the order. As soon as one prospect closed and became a customer, they would erase the name and replace it. It was low-tech, but it kept them focused on what they needed to do on any given day.

Do you go to work every day with a clear plan of what must be done to close business already in the cycle? Do you know the activities that need to be done to replace that prospect when you close the sale? If the answer is NO, then write down your current pipeline on paper or put one into your computer today.

This is the first step to jumpstarting your activity and ultimately your success. Remember, an organized sales person is an efficient sales person. If you don't manage your pipeline properly, there's a big probability that you'll lose track of a potential customer. Unless you have a secretary that handles everything for you--which you probably don't since you're a budding sales professional reading this book--you have to develop a system that allows you to keep track of who's who.

Always find ways of streamlining your pipeline handling process. Go old-school if you have to. But do not let your Pipeline become disorganized.

Think of your pipeline as the life blood that allows you to live. If you're bleeding all over the place, chances are high that you'll die due to loss of blood. Same principle applies in sales. If your pipeline is disorganized, you can be rest assured that your business will soon die.

Chapter 4 - Treat the Prospect or Customer with Importance

How do you really view the person you're dealing with across the desk, the conference table, or the phone? Is he just another someone you can make a buck by selling to, or does he represent a person with a problem which you can help solve? Are you really focused on him, or in making the sale and spending the commission?

In survey after survey, the number one complaint from the customers is that of rudeness, inefficiency, or just plain indifference. Two of these have to do with simple human relations; how we feel. Our attitude about our prospects and customers comes out loud and clear in our actions.

The Forum Corporation studied high and low performance sales people. One of their discoveries was that the high performing sales people took just as much time and effort with their internal customer--those inside their organization--as with their external customers. Most salespeople's success depend upon people to whom they have little or no supervisory control. High performing sales people understand that respect and a positive attitude towards those on shipping, installation, service, and administration will help them satisfy the external customer, and possibly lead to more sales and referrals.

You see, making a serious effort to keep your customers makes good economic sense. It cost more to bring in a new customer than it does to keep a current customer. It cost more time, effort, as well as marketing dollars. Also, if that customer leaves disgruntled, he'll tell an average of 11 other people about the problem he had with you and your organization.

What most novice sales professional fail to realize is that it'll take more time and effort to appease a disgruntled customer than to develop and maintain a good relationship with one. This is the reason why companies spend millions of dollars in customer retention via their customer service department.

Therefore, a high performing sales person does not think in terms of replacing customers. Instead, he or she thinks in terms of maintaining customers and adding new ones in order to build his or her business bigger and better. In order to be a successful sales person, be sensitive to the value of the customer's time.

Because you've spent more time planning your strategy and preparing for the call, spend more quality time in front of the customer. Customers perceive this and will value it highly. Become aware of the personal pressures and needs faced by the customers and sell the people, not the company.

Take time to build relationships with both your internal and external customers.

Relationship is what makes a customer come back to you again and again to buy more products or services. If the customer encounters problems at any stage of the sales process, be quick to come to their rescue and help them move towards completing the sales. Show the prospect or customer that they are important no matter the size of the business pie they are bringing into your company.

Show Your Willingness and Intent to Help

Sales managers and sales professionals often get caught up in the sales skills trap in trying to find the secret or missing ingredient to their sales process. They focus on sales techniques, when in fact, they should be focused on intent. As what many successful sales veterans say, "you can have everything in this life that you want as long as you help enough people to get what they want."

The goal of a true selling professional is to help their prospects and their customers get what they want, and more importantly, what they need. The key is to remember that intent is more important than technique. In other words, your desire to help is far more important than knowing fourteen different ways to close a sale.

So how do you demonstrate your desire and your intent to help your prospects and customers? Well, for starters, try this: Before launching into your probing questions to uncover any need for your product or service, begin by framing the sales call first. After the warm-up or initial small talk and greetings, try a statement like this:

> *"Thank you again for your time today and having us here. We really have a simple agenda for today's meeting. First, we would like to know more about you, your role, and some of the projects and initiatives you're currently working on. Secondly, we will share a little bit about ourselves; the company and what we do. And lastly, if it's appropriate and make sense, we can look together at action items or next steps. Does that sound fair?"*

More than likely, your prospect or customer will say, "Yes. Of course, it sounds fair." They may add to the agenda or do a time check, but they will usually agree that it's a fair way to begin a meeting. Now, let's analyze the wording.

You ask permission to learn more about them, then share a little about you. More them, little you. Then you use the words "we," "us," and "together." When they agree that the agenda sounds fair, they have agreed to allow you to ask questions first and learn more about them.

By asking relevant questions and taking the time to understand their business needs, you'll have moved from a vendor relationship to more of a partner or consulting relationship. This path will certainly help you demonstrate your intent and desire to help your prospects and customers find the solutions they truly need. Once you've expressed your sincerest intent and desire to help them address an ongoing or impending issue, then they'll be more interested on what you have to say about how your product or service can benefit them.

To implement this technique successfully, write down the sentences we used previously to frame the sales call on an index card. Review it until you can say it conversationally and comfortably. You will find that people are interested in talking about themselves and their situations, which then gives you the information you need to help solve their problems. Express your intent, uncover their need, and then close the sale.

Make a Positive First Impression

People, including your prospects and customers, will take from 3 to 30 seconds to make a decision about whether they want to give you their time and attention. Once the impression has been made, all the information will be filtered through that initial decision. How can you and your company make a positive first impression, and then build on that to establish trust and rapport? Let's first look at your company.

When someone is coming to your establishment to do business, what do they see? They begin to form opinions about your business before they talk to a single person. Is the building neat and clean? Is the reception area projecting the right image for your business?

Take a look at your physical surroundings through the eyes of the prospect. Is it making the best first impression? Maybe your prospect's first contact with your company is over the phone. Is it answered properly? Do they have to go through a series of impersonal voicemail options before getting to a live person?

Maybe your prospect's first contact is through the mail. Are your company's marketing pieces professional? Are they well written and well designed? You may have little or no input into how your company forms an impression for the prospect. So, let's turn our attention onto what you can control--YOU personally.

How do you create a positive first impression? Just as a prospect may make an impression of your business from the outside, we'll also form an impression of you based on your "outside." Are you clean, neat, warm, and friendly?

Also, think about your business card. When you hand it to someone, does it make the right impression? Keep the design simple. Use the front of your card to display your contact information only. Use the back of the card to give your company's mission statement, a map to your office, a list of products and services you can offer, anything that is helpful to the prospect.

However, beware. As important as first impressions can be, the most current contact the person has had with you or your company will be the freshest thing on their mind. So start strong with a positive first impression, but remain strong with consistent follow-up, attention to service, and a focus on solving the prospect's needs and wants.

To be able to make a first impression right now, take inventory of all the opportunities you have to contact a prospect, your physical building, your marketing materials, your business card, and most importantly, YOU the sales person. What kind of impression are you making? What can you do to improve the impression you are making?

Strive to make the best impression possible because people like to buy from people they trust. Make every effort to express your sincere trustworthiness and you will make a positive lasting impression. Remember, good impressions is what makes a recurring customer. The good thing about a recurring customer is that you don't have to look for them. They will be the one to proactively look for you and give you their business.

Chapter 5 - Making Use of Elevator Statements

When you get the familiar question, "What do you do?" how do you answer? If you answer with a job description like, "Oh, I'm in sales for the Siemens Company," then you are not using that opportunity to prospect. What you want is a statement that makes the listener intrigued, and is prompted to ask you more.

These statements are basically called elevator statements. The reason why they are called as such is because they have to be fast enough, and noteworthy enough to pique someone's interest in the time it takes to ride an elevator. A good statement needs to be short, about a key benefit, and said with sincerity. If you have limited time with someone, it will help that you establish credibility quickly, and hopefully get the potential prospect interested to hear more. Some examples of elevator statements are:

- What do you do? I build better business by building better individuals.

- What do you do? We provide the keys to the American dream of owning a home.

- What do you do? We work with clients that have a passion to increase their business while creating more family time.

Each of these examples give just enough information for the prospect to want to know how, why or what you're talking about. You use elevator statements if you're meeting someone in a quick setting; an airport, a chamber of commerce meeting, or any place that you can get the question, "What do you do?"

To effectively pique your prospects interest, brainstorm some quick, clever statements that describe what you do in terms of a benefit. To do that, ask yourself what you like best about the product, the service, or the company you work for. It's a good place to begin describing your job in terms of what you can do for others.

One of the National Guard recruiters was asked what he does for a living. And he said that he helps young people attain their dreams. That reply would certainly get a conversation going. It will allow the recruiter to expand on the benefits of college tuition, paid training, and many other benefits of joining the U.S. Army National Guard.

Create two or three of these elevator statements and practice using them to become comfortable and effective at using every opportunity as a prospecting opportunity. By now, it would have dawned on you that the key to prospecting is learning how to hook the prospect in; raising their curiosity about you and what you have to offer. The elevator statement is designed to do just that.

Once you hook the prospect in, you have every opportunity to probe and uncover their need, and presenting the benefit of the product or service that you're offering in relation to that need. And with a little bit of objection handling skills--if there are any objections by the prospect at all--you'll surely convince the prospect that they indeed need what you're offering. Once the groundwork has been laid, you can now ask to close the sales.

Utilizing General Benefit Statements

When you want to capture the attention of a prospect, you can use a general benefit statement. Now this statement is longer than the elevator statement that we just finished discussing. It's used when you're calling on a list of people in which you want to generate interest in talking to further.

It's also when you call and leave a voicemail message. This statement will increase your chances of a successful first contact. It will also give the prospect a reason for meeting or talking with you. In other words, it creates value. General benefit statements include three parts: your competitive advantage, a sales objective, and a brief information point about the prospect.

Your competitive advantage is a benefit that your product or service has over the competition. While you don't know this prospect yet, or if this benefit is specific to the prospect, you do know that this is a general benefit that most prospects are drawn to. Therefore, you need to do some thinking, some research, and some comparison to your competition.

What does your product or service have that others don't have? Is your warranty better, or does your product save more time? Does it have less maintenance cost, or does your company provide superior technical follow-up, better service, or cheaper installation? This competitive advantage is a great way to leverage yourself into an appointment with that prospect.

Once you get to know the prospect's situation a little better, you can then target the features and benefits that fit directly to the prospect. For now, you are just trying to win the opportunity to talk further with the person. Next, you want to state your objectives to the prospect clearly.

It could be many things. For instance, you may be calling to secure an appointment, introduce your new product, or set a follow-up phone call. You need to know why you're calling so the prospect can know why you're calling. The last part of your statement is to let the prospect know that you've done a little research and you know a little about him or her. Give the feeling that you're interested enough to have done some homework. If you're reaching the prospect for the first time, say something like this:

> *"Hello Mr. Stewart. My name is Rick Grimes. I represent the Ney*

York Marketing Initiative. I'm calling because the Bellagio is very similar to another hotel property in New York that we've been helping to increase their guest retention. Recently, this client of ours realized that there's a 37% increase in return customers using our program. Now, since you're the director of guest services at the Bellagio, I assume that you're under constant competitive pressure, is that right? If there were a way I could help you relieve that pressure, would you be interested in meeting with me? Well, that's great. I think a 20 minute appointment would be a perfect starting point to see if what we offer is something your hotel could use to increase your occupancy.

I'm open on Mondays thru Fridays. Which would work for you?"

Be a 'Curious' Salesperson

Questions allow us to gather information that enables us to help our clients. And just as important is when we ask questions in a professional manner. By asking questions in a professional manner, we establish the most important thing in the sales process; trust.

When you ask questions in a sinccre manner, you are showing that you are truly interested in the prospect's best interest. Properly worded questions are the best way to discover the true needs of a prospect or client. Questions demonstrate that the purpose of your call is to find the prospect's needs and interest while gathering information. You do this so that both you and the prospect can learn how your products and services can benefit their needs.

Prospects like to be heard in order to have the confidence that you really do understand that their situation is different. In reality, their situation may not be different. But reality, like beauty, is in the eye of the beholder. When can never gain the trust of prospects until they believe we are really interested in solving their "unique" problem.

We are not suggesting that you ask a series of questions that feels like an interrogation; or questions so obvious that you are leading them down a specific path. Instead, what we're suggesting is that you ask questions that combine both the emotion and the logic. Use thinking and feeling questions. Questions phrased with, "How do you feel about it?" will help you learn how the customer feels. After that, you are more likely to find out what that person thinks.

There are two aspects of the mind that you want to combine; logic and emotion. The one that prompts the prospect to make that buying decision is emotion. Logic, on the other hand, allows them to make that justification on the purchase that they've made afterwards.

Be sure to ask more open-ended questions than close-ended questions. Open-ended questions are those most valuable types of questions that you can ask, since they allow the prospect to give you the most information about themselves and their issues. They begin with words like, "What," "How," "Why," "When," or "Tell me more about that."

Close-ended questions, on the other hand, can be answered with a simple yes or no. Use them to gather facts. They should be used infrequently during the sales process. You can also ask reflective questions. They give you a chance to reflect on a previous comment and give the prospect a chance to elaborate on clarity.

A question that begins with, "What do you mean by...?" or "How is that impacting your business?" are examples of follow-up questions to the prospect's previous answer. You will also want to occasionally use a direct agreement question. Direct agreement questions are yes-no-type answered questions that you already know the answer to before you ask them.

For example, "This would save you time, wont it?" This gets the prospect into an agreeing mode. The agreeing mode helps you sell later on. To apply these types of questions properly, write down sample questions you could use with your next prospect or customer. Then work some of those questions into your conversations to see how they can work for you.

Chapter 6 - Always Have a 'Closing' Attitude

If you want to be a successful sales person, you must develop a "closing" attitude. Another name for closing could be "need satisfaction." It's what you have been building up to do.

You offer your product or service as they need solution. Closing sales doesn't have to be painful for you or the prospect. In fact, it is a win-win situation if you've done everything for the benefit of the prospect.

Asking for the order is the natural progression that must occur. In sales, not asking for the sale is like running to the half-way mark of a marathon and then quitting. If you've already sourced a prospect, developed rapport, established trust, uncovered the need, and presented your product, why not go all the way and ask for the sale?

By not asking for the sale, you've wasted your time and effort in laying the groundwork for the whole sales call. Asking for the sale is the final stage of any sales presentation.

Ask for the sale pleasantly and professionally. The proper approach in following these suggestions will put you in a win-win situation. This means that you have now reached an agreement with the prospect and you clearly understand that the sales process is something you do for a person and not to that person.

The closing attitude is your understanding that you are there to solve a problem, or prevent some in the future. Not closing the sale will also give the prospect an impression that you're not sincere in helping them solve their problem. You just went there, told them what they wanted to hear, and then stepped away as if you've changed your mind.

Not asking for the sale is considered taboo in the world of sales. Why in the world would you go into the selling business if you have no intention of asking for the sale--selling--in the first place?

To develop a closing attitude, realize that regardless of circumstances, technical knowledge, experience, investment, or anything else, always ask for the order. Don't be afraid, or even be ashamed, to ask for the sale. If your prospect says no, the reason is most often that they do not know enough to say yes. In that case, you begin the process of managing objections.

How do you effectively manage objections? You go and ask the prospect questions. In addition, you can also present them with new evidence and information in order for them to make a new buying decision. Go out there with a positive attitude and make those sales.

Keep your enthusiasm up at all times. There may come a time when you would feel down about losing a prospect or a customer. Don't let disappointments pull you down. Shrug the disappointment off and proceed with the next prospect on the list.

Do not waste your time dwelling on failures. Instead keep moving and focus on the next sale. Keep the mistakes that you've made in the past, if there are any, and then make sure you don't commit them on the next sales call that you make. Remember, nothing happens until somebody sells something. Let that person be you.

Learn to Try More than Five Times to Ask for the Sale

So, what keeps you from closing? Research from Dr. Herbert Williams of Harvard reveals that 46% of the sales people he interviewed asked for the order once, and then quit. 24% asked for the order twice before giving up. 14% asked the third time. And 12 % hanged in there to make the four attempts before throwing in the proverbial towel.

That's a total of 96% who quit after four closing attempts. And yet the same research shows that a full 60% of all sales are made after the fifth closing attempt. How many times do you attempt to close the sale before you leave? If the answer isn't five, then you may need to go back and try again.

For those of you who are reluctant to ask for the order more than once or twice for fear of coming across as high-pressure sales people, think about this: When baseball pitchers reject the ball, the ball is returned to the umpire who puts it in his pouch with the other baseballs. Later, that same ball would be given to the pitcher.

Seldom, if ever, is the same ball rejected twice. In the same way, the prospect will look at your offer in a different light; the second, third, forth, and even the fifth time. Just as a professional baseball umpire offers the same baseball to the pitcher, so must the professional sales person offer the same product to the prospect several times. Asking your prospect for the order more than four times can be exceptionally tough if you:

> a.) don't believe in the service or product that you sell

b.) didn't go through the initial sales process steps properly

c.) don't even expect to make the sale at all

Note that between each closing effort, you must give additional reasons, features, functions, and benefits for the prospect to make the "Yes" decision today. When you offer added information, you allow the prospect to make a new decision based on additional information.

Many times we don't ask the question because we don't want to hear the "No." This is where you'll want to give yourself a gut check. To do this, you need to debrief each sales call immediately after the presentation. That is, get alone and relive the experience.

This is most effective when you keep a written journal of your observations. Ask yourself, "Did I ask for the order? If not, why?" If some of your answers are, "..the timing just wasn't right," "The prospect was distracted," "..there were too many people around," or "..she needed to take a breather and think things through," realize these are often excuses for not asking for the order.

Don't misunderstand. There are occasions when it's wise to back away and return another day, especially if the amount of investment you're asking the prospect to make is significant. However, in an overwhelming majority of the cases, you need to be honest with yourself and admit you're just making excuses for yourself and you need to ask for the order.

To learn how to ask for the order every time, count how many times you asked for the order with each prospect today. If it's less than five, then tomorrow, commit to yourself that you'll just try one more time with each prospect.

Make Use of the 3 Reliable 'Asking for the Sale' Closes

Although there are literally hundreds of ways to ask for the order, we will be sharing a few from the field that are tested and reliable. It is good if you know lots of different closes. But do you know them well enough to use them at a moment's notice in the proper sales environment?

The point here is to learn and practice many different kinds of closes. However, make sure you know them well and can use them for the genuine good of the prospect. The key is this: don't reinvent the wheel.

Educate yourself on other people's experiences. After working with these closes a while, you will be able to personalize them and make them fit your sales presentation. The first close is the "Three questions" close. You use these three simple questions:

1. *"Can you see where this would..?"* and you insert the primary

benefit that would cause the prospect to buy.

2. *"Are you interested in..?"* then you state the benefit again.

3. *"If you were ever going to start this benefit, when do you think would be the best time to start?"*

If you have made your presentation in such a way that you can expect an affirmative answer to the first question, then the process would work for you. It helps you tie the emotion of the decision to the logic of the decision. In the second question, what you may want to try is the probability close.

Once your prospect is at the moment of truth, you may ask a following question to obtain the order or the information you need to get the order. Remember to choose your words carefully. You don't want to plant seeds of disinterest or the impression of falling for anything.

Wait patiently for the response. This close is best used when you are very close to getting the order, but feel there's some resistance you need to get into the open. Handling this resistance or objection gets the problem into the open and enables you to deal with each one properly.

Finally, the summary close is a good basic close to know and use. Even though it may seem very basic to you, don't minimize the significance of what may seem obvious. In the summary close, you recap the areas of the presentation that caused the light bulb on your prospect's head to light up, and then ask for your order.

After you receive a favorable reply, you definitely should go for the close and say, "..then let's get the order started." You see, during the sales process, the prospect gets excited about certain benefits you can provide. But during the sales process, that excitement may begin to die down due to any number of circumstances or directions.

By summarizing, you rekindle the flame at the moment you're asking the prospect to make their investment. The more "feeling" they have at this moment, the more sales you will close. To successfully implement this technique in your sales process, take each of these three closes and work on making it fit your personality, your product, or service, and then practice, practice, practice. You will be sure to close more sales more often with practiced closes that you can deliver with confidence and ease.

Conclusion

Thank you for taking the time to read this book on the art of selling. We hope that we've imparted some useful skills in order for you to make your sales career better. From this point onwards, start applying everything that you've learned in this book. Take this book as a beginners guide on how to be effective at selling.

Lastly, keep in mind that a sales person is not in the selling business. A sales person is in the people business. Try to impart the knowledge that you've learned in this book so that we may all have a wonderful and fruitful sales career. There's no better feeling than being able to help another person become a great sales person.

Thank you very much and may you have more sales to come.

www.ingramcontent.com/pod-product-compliance
Lightning Source LLC
Chambersburg PA
CBHW070327190526
45169CB00005B/1780